The Natural History Museum
Weird & Wonderful Guides

Scary
and
Sneaky

Barbara Taylor

OXFORD
UNIVERSITY PRESS

OXFORD
UNIVERSITY PRESS

Great Clarendon Street, Oxford OX2 6DP

Oxford University Press is a department of the University of Oxford.
It furthers the University's objective of excellence in research, scholarship,
and education by publishing worldwide in

Oxford New York

Athens Auckland Bangkok Bogotá Buenos Aires
Cape Town Chennai Dar es Salaam Delhi Florence Hong Kong Istanbul
Karachi Kolkata Kuala Lumpur Madrid Melbourne Mexico City Mumbai
Nairobi Paris São Paulo Shanghai Singapore Taipei Tokyo Toronto Warsaw

with associated companies in Berlin Ibadan

Oxford is a registered trade mark of Oxford University Press
in the UK and in certain other countries

British Library Cataloguing in Publication Data available

Hardback ISBN 0-19-910676 2
Paperback ISBN 0-19-910837 4

1 3 5 7 9 10 8 6 4 2

Printed in Hong Kong

Acknowledgments

The publishers would like to thank:
Marwell Zoological Park, National Birds of Prey Centre, Weymouth Sealife Park, Chelsea
Physic Garden, Kings Reptile World, Virginia Cheeseman, Mark O'Shea and the following
staff at The Natural History Museum, London: Barry Bolton, Steve Brooks, Paul Clark,
Barry Clarke, Paul Cornelius, Oliver Crimmen, Peter Forey, Frank Greenaway, Richard
Harbord, Daphne Hills, Paul Hillyard, Paula Jenkins, Carol Levick, Judith Marshall, Colin
McCarthy, Angela Milner, Fred Naggs, Cally Oldershaw, Gordon Paterson, Robert Press,
Robert Prys-Jones, Gaden Robinson, Andrew Smith, Chris Stanley, Frank Steinheimer,
John Taylor, Kathie Way, the staff of the EM Unit, Photo Unit, Picture Library
and Publishing Division.

The creatures in this book are not reproduced life size, or to scale.

All photos reproduced by kind permission of The Natural History Museum
with the exception of the following:
Science Photo Library: p14bl (Claude Nuridsany & Marie Perennoli); p16b (Kraft Explorer)
Oxford Scientific Films: p17
BBC Natural History Unit: p20tr (Premaphotos)
The illustration on p14c is by Steve Roberts.

Contents

Terrors and tricks

Razor-sharp teeth, ENORMOUS bodies, deadly poisons, painful stings, electric shocks, clever tricks, vast numbers ... these are the things that can make animals scary and sneaky. In the wild, being scary or sneaky helps an animal to survive an attack, or catch its food.

Scorpions sting to defend themselves and to kill their prey.

A scorpion's sting is a hollow tube on the end of its tail, connected to a bag of poison. Muscles squeeze poison from the bag down the tube and into the victim. Some scorpions can kill people.

The terrifying teeth of a Siberian tiger sink into its prey like daggers. Its huge front paws, with their sharp claws, knock the prey over and hold on tight.

The wolfish uses its strong, curved fangs for crunching through the shells of crabs, mussels and sea urchins.

7

Did You Know ?

One Brazilian wandering spider holds enough poison to kill 225 mice.

Electric eels can stun a person, or kill fishes and frogs, with electric shocks.

Giant pythons can kill and eat leopards.

Green poison dart frogs make deadly poisons in their skin to keep them safe from predators. Their bright colours warn predators that they're poisonous.

The ink comes from large bags attached to the cuttlefish's gut.

When attacked, cuttlefish squirt out clouds of black ink. This acts like a smoke screen to confuse predators and give the cuttlefish time to escape.

Poisons and stings

Beware the blue-ringed octopus! The poisonous saliva of just one octopus can paralyse 10 people, although its poison is usually used to kill crabs. Many creatures use poisons, to catch food or to defend themselves. Stings, spines or sharp beaks help to deliver the poison.

The long tentacles of this spotted jellyfish are armed with lots of stinging cells. Jellyfish are slow movers, but their nasty stings help to protect them from their enemies.

Try not to step on one of these weever fish when you are paddling in the sea! They hide in the sand near the shore and have spines on the small black fin to inject poison.

Can you see the
razor-sharp spine sticking
out of this stingray's tail? It is
full of poison. Stingrays lash
out with their tails if they are
disturbed or attacked.

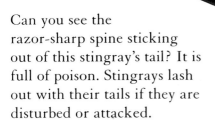

The circles turn a brighter blue when the octopus is threatened.

The bright colours
of the blue-ringed
octopus carry a warning
message: Keep away,
I am deadly poisonous!

Only female wasps can sting,
because the sting is made from
an egg-laying tool and only
females lay eggs. Wasps can
take their poisonous sting out
of a victim and use it again.

Did You Know ?

A honey bee can usually
only sting once.

A box jellyfish can sting a person
to death in less than five minutes.

Some cone shells kill fish
with a poisonous dart.

Terrible teeth

We use knives and forks to cut up our food, which we 'catch' in the supermarket. But in the wild, meat-eating animals use their terrible teeth to catch their meals and tear them up into bite-sized chunks. They also use their teeth to defend themselves from enemies.

This Mexican cantil has poisonous fangs that fold back inside the roof of its mouth. Poison flows down the hollow fangs, from tiny bags just behind the eyes, and comes out of a hole near the tips.

The long, fragile canine teeth of sabre-toothed cats were used to stab their victims through the throat. They could even kill the elephants that lived alongside them, up to two million years ago.

There was a gap in the lower jaw to make room for the huge fangs above.

Sawfish slash their incredibly sharp noses from side to side, to kill their prey and to defend themselves from enemies.

Tiger fish have sharp, pointed teeth, like tigers, and black stripes too. New teeth grow to replace their old ones.

Did You Know ?

A bite from the cantil's poisonous fangs can kill a person.

Teeth developed out of bony armour near the mouths of armoured fish.

An elephant's tusks are long top front teeth.

This pig's tusk is a lower canine tooth, curved upwards.

This fossil tooth of an ancient megalodon shark is about as big as a child's hand. These fierce sharks probably used their teeth for slashing deep into large prey, like great white sharks do today.

11

This giant crocodile had massive jaws full of sharp teeth. It is an ancient species, which lived 83-71 million years ago. It may have attacked dinosaurs at the water's edge.

The crocodile's name, *Deinosuchus*, means 'terror crocodile'.

Night-time terrors

With strange sounds and spooky shadows, the night can seem scary to us. Yet many creatures come out at night because they can hide from enemies in the darkness. Their special eyes, ears, and other senses help them find their way and spot a snack.

At night, the pupils in the middle of this viper's eyes open wide to let in as much light as possible. It uses its forked tongue to pick up smells from the air.

Special heat holes on the face detect heat given off by warm prey.

Barn owls swoop down on mice and voles like silent white ghosts. Their sharp talons kill like a ring of tiny spears.

Did You Know ?

A vampire bat drinks about four teaspoonfuls of blood a day.

The roar of a male lion at night can be heard 4 km away.

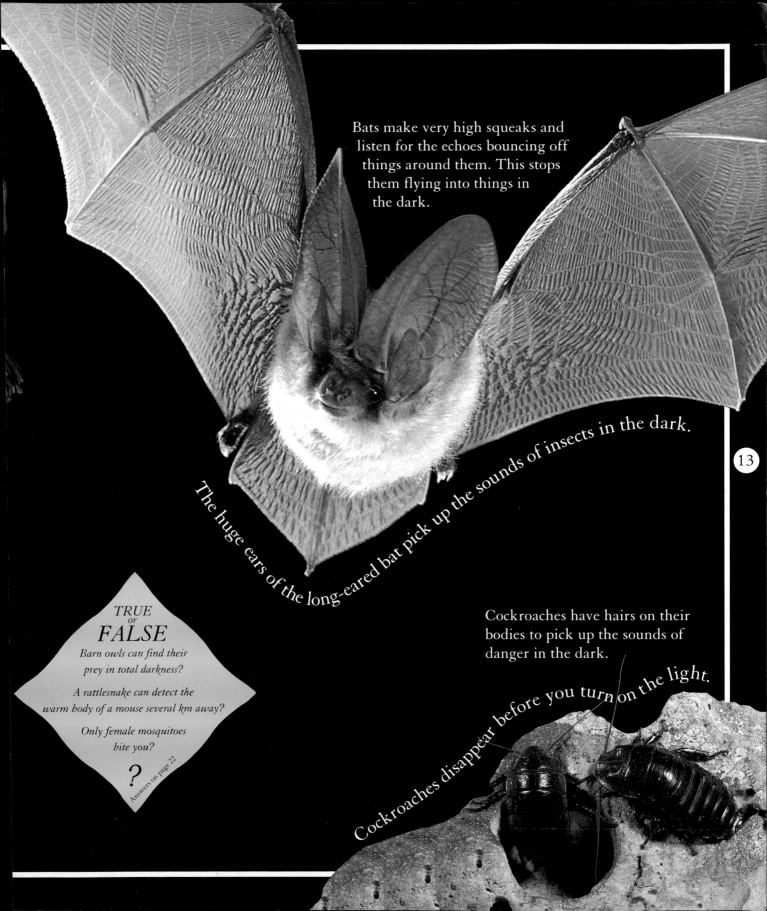

Bats make very high squeaks and listen for the echoes bouncing off things around them. This stops them flying into things in the dark.

The huge ears of the long-eared bat pick up the sounds of insects in the dark.

13

TRUE
or
FALSE

Barn owls can find their prey in total darkness?

A rattlesnake can detect the warm body of a mouse several km away?

Only female mosquitoes bite you?

?

Answers on page 22

Cockroaches have hairs on their bodies to pick up the sounds of danger in the dark.

Cockroaches disappear before you turn on the light.

Plant attack!

Did you know that some plants can trap and eat small animals? These plants often grow in poor soils, and so the animals' bodies give them extra goodness. Other plants defend themselves from animal attacks with stings and sharp spines.

Snap! An insect brushes against the hairs on the leaves of a Venus flytrap, and they snap shut. The spikes on the leaves work like prison bars.

Flies beware! Pitcher plants attract insects to their hollow leaves, with their bright colours and nectar. Once the insects slide down inside the pitcher, they cannot get out. They drown in a pool of water and digestive juices.

Pitchers develop from the tips of leaves that swell up and fill with air.

Sundew leaves have hairs with sticky 'glue' on the ends. Insects are attracted, thinking it's food, but then get completely stuck. The leaves curl around them and start to digest their meal.

Ouch! Hairs on nettle leaves pierce your skin and give you an injection of poison. No wonder it hurts! Each hair can only sting once, then it falls off the plant.

The nettle's stinging hairs can only be seen clearly with a magnifying glass.

Did You Know ?

Some pitcher plants eat mice, frogs and scorpions.

A Venus flytrap takes 8-20 days to eat an insect.

Only one cactus grows outside America in the wild.

Any animal trying to eat this cactus would get a mouthful of sharp spines! The spines are the plant's leaves, and they lose less water than wide, flat leaves.

Scary surprises

Powerful forces deep inside the
Earth or high in the sky can be
super-scary. Volcanoes, earthquakes
and avalanches destroy buildings as
easily as if they were toys. And it's
hard to predict exactly when they
will happen. We can tell when a
storm is brewing, but not where
the lightning will strike!

Whoosh! The spectacular fountains
that burst out of volcanoes are liquid,
red-hot rocks from inside the Earth,
escaping through a crack like a fizzy
drink spurting out of a can.

Lightning heats up the air quickly, making it spread out suddenly at supersonic speed. We hear the speeding air as the crash and bang of thunder.

Zap! A gigantic spark of electricity zig-zags betweeen thunderclouds and the ground. Lightning is a way of releasing energy that builds up inside the cloud.

Did You Know ?

Volcanic lava can flow at up to 60 km per hour.

Lightning heats up the air to a temperature hotter than the surface of the Sun.

There are ten times more active volcanoes under the sea than on land.

Clever tricks

Can you imagine a fish that puffs itself up like a football? Animals use all sorts of clever tricks to make sure they stay alive as long as possible, or catch a juicy meal. Some even pretend to be dead, because predators prefer to eat their food while it's still alive - yuk!

Puffers have poisonous insides but are safe to touch.

Hermit crabs are not like other crabs. They have a soft tail and so they have to sneak inside empty seashells for protection.

By puffing itself up with water or air, this puffer fish quickly turns itself into a spiky ball too big and prickly for predators to swallow.

TRUE or FALSE

A sea cucumber squirts out its insides to save its own skin?

Octopuses turn blue when they are scared?

A starfish can grow a new tail?

?

Answers on page 22

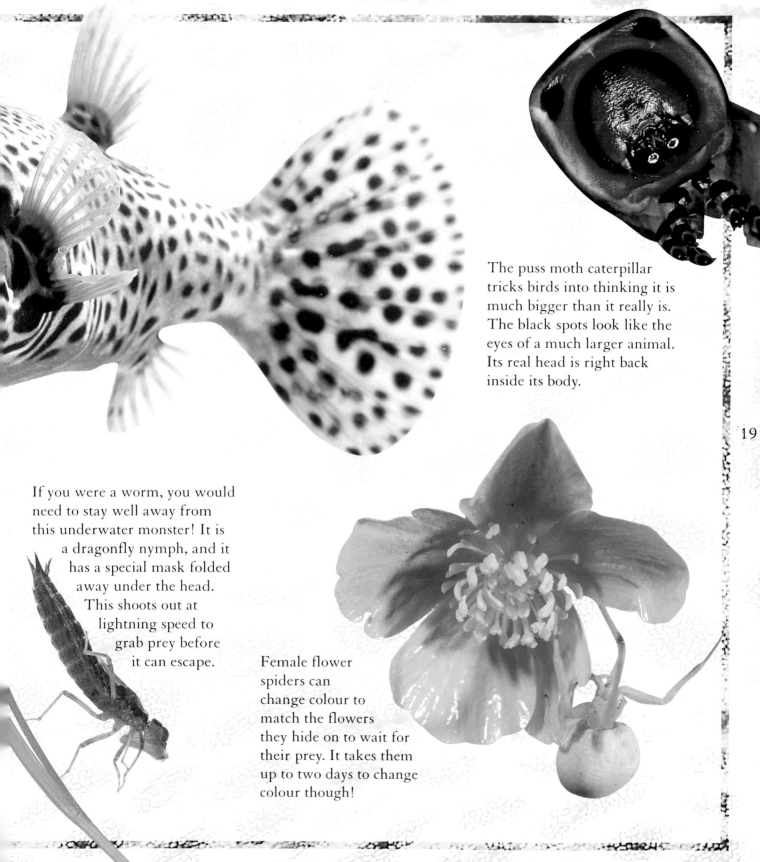

The puss moth caterpillar tricks birds into thinking it is much bigger than it really is. The black spots look like the eyes of a much larger animal. Its real head is right back inside its body.

If you were a worm, you would need to stay well away from this underwater monster! It is a dragonfly nymph, and it has a special mask folded away under the head. This shoots out at lightning speed to grab prey before it can escape.

Female flower spiders can change colour to match the flowers they hide on to wait for their prey. It takes them up to two days to change colour though!

Disguises and armour

Animals are way ahead of people when it comes to survival. Their suits of armour fit them better than a glove. Their camouflaged clothing makes them almost invisible. And their disguises turn them into secret agents that are impossible to detect.

This looks like an ant, but they only have six legs and this creature has eight. Spiders have eight legs, so this must be a spider, disguised as an ant! Predators avoid an ant's nasty sting.

The suit of armour is made up of tough scales set in the thick leathery skin.

A caiman's body is covered in protective scales - rather like the coats of chain mail worn by medieval knights long ago. The caiman cannot take its coat off, but it can grow new scales to replace old and damaged ones.

The leafy sea dragon cannot make a quick getaway from danger. Instead, it relies on truly wonderful camouflage: it grows pretend seaweed all over its body, that disguises its real shape.

Spiny stick insects blend in so well with a background of prickly stems that it's hard to see where the stem ends and the insect starts!

Did You Know?

Seahorses can change colour to match the background.

Some grasshoppers look like stick insects for extra protection.

Some spiders are disguised by looking like bird droppings.

Index

True or False answers

Night-time terrors
★ True, they use their excellent hearing to find their prey.
★ False, from about 30 cm away.
★ True, females need blood to help their eggs develop.

Clever tricks
★ True, it grows new insides in a few months.
★ False, they turn blue or a darker colour when they're
  angry, and white or a lighter colour when they're scared.
★ False, it can grow new arms, but it doesn't have a tail.

23